October 25, 1986

October 25, 1986

First English edition published by Colour Library Books Ltd.
© 1984 Illustrations by London Features International, London,
Rex Features, London and Gamma/Paris.
© 1984 Text by Colour Library Books Ltd., Guildford, Surrey, England.
This edition published by Greenwich House, a division of Arlington House, Inc.,
distributed by Crown Publishers, Inc.
h g f e d c b a
Text filmsetting and color separations by Llovet, Barcelona, Spain.

Printed and bound in Barcelona, Spain,
by JISA-RIEUSSET and EUROBINDER.

ISBN 0 517 451484
GREENWICH HOUSE

MICHAEL JACKSON

by Stewart Regan

Designed by
Philip Clucas MSIAD

Produced by
**Ted Smart and
David Gibbon**

GREENWICH HOUSE

"All children, except one, grow up."

This is the opening sentence of Michael Jackson's favorite book "Peter Pan", J.M. Barrie's immortal children's classic. And it's a line that strikes a chord inside his heart.

While he has taken the world by storm with his classic Jackson 5 records, his Grammy award winning solo albums 'Off The Wall' and 'Thriller', his stunningly charismatic videos of 'Billie Jean', 'Beat It', and 'Thriller' and his record breaking singles success, he is a shy and solitary man.

He lives with his mother and two younger sisters in Encino, California. While the whole family is independent, Michael admits he couldn't leave home.

"I think I'd die on my own. I'd be so lonely. Even at home, I'm lonely. I sit in my room sometimes and cry. It's so hard to make friends, and there are some things you can't talk to your parents or family about.

"I sometimes walk around the neighborhood at night, just hoping to find someone to talk to. But I end up coming home."

The lightning bolt of energy that burst onto the pop scene in 1970 with the worldwide smash single 'I Want You Back' and entranced the world over the past 14 years, is the most famous young man in the world.

It so nearly never happened. Joe Jackson had a dream. He wanted to be a star musician –a guitarist. But before he and wife Katherine had turned around, their modest house in Gary, Indiana was filled with hungry mouths.

First came Maureen (Rebbie). She was quickly followed by Sigmund (Jackie), Toriano (Tito), Jermaine, LaToya, Marlon, Michael, Steven (Randy) and Janet.

Joe had been singing and playing in a band called the Falcons, but without much success. Joe knew he had to put both the dream and the guitar on the shelf and put his back into raising his family.

Working as a crane operator in the bleak landscape of Gary's factory belt, his dream must have seemed far out of reach. Luckily his guitar wasn't so inaccessible to other eager hands.

It was Tito's young fingers that caressed Joe's prize possession while Pa Jackson was out. One day Tito played the treasured instrument once too often and found the stern, authoritarian figure of his father standing over him.

Michael recalls the incident: "My father got mad", he says, "so angry and he said, 'Tito, sit down. I wanna see if you can play that guitar. If you can't, I'm really gonna beat you.' "

Under threat of the belt, Tito played.

"My father was shocked", continues Michael, "he saw some special talent there. He was really surprised, and he was so happy his son could do this."

Soon the three eldest boys, Jackie, Tito and Jermaine, were being taught the basics. As soon as they were old enough Marlon and Michael were drafted into the group; Michael was an apple-cheeked dynamo who pounded the bongos.

But there was something special about him.

One day Katherine Jackson was surprised to hear baby Michael imitating Jermaine's lead vocal in his clear, toddler's falsetto. She told her husband, "I think we have another lead singer!"

The brothers agreed. Jackie recalls: "He was so energetic that at five years old, he was like a leader, we saw that. So, we said, 'Hey, Michael, you be the lead guy'.

"The audience ate it up. He was into those James Brown things at the time, you know. The speed was the thing. He would see somebody do something, and he could do it right away."

His mother agrees: "It was sort of frightening. He was so young. He didn't go

out and play much. So, if you want me to
tell the truth, I don't know where he got it.
He just knew."

What was clear was that Michael Joseph
Jackson's voice was going to be heard way
beyond Gary, Indiana.

Joe Jackson realized he had hot property
on his hands and vigorously encouraged his
sons. His money was used to buy them
instruments, much against the initial
wishes of his wife, Katherine.

Joe admitted later, "We went overboard.
My wife and I would fight, because I
invested in new instruments that cost so
much. When a woman's a good mother and
finds all the money going into instruments,
she doesn't like it."

Jermaine recalls, "Even before our
record contract we were always sheltered,
Mommy and Daddy's babes. We used to
have to be in before the street lights were
lit. We missed out on our childhoods. We
were always having to rehearse when the
other kids would come around and ask us
to come out and play.

"We loved going to school", he reveals,
"because it was the only time we could play
and let off steam doing things like physical
education."

In 1965, seven-year-old Michael went on
stage for the first time with his brothers –a
talent show at a local high school. The
Jackson 5 sang The Temptations' classic
'My Girl' and won.

"I was scared, of course", remembers
Michael. "I was scared to let the people see
me sing. They might 'boo' us. They might
not like us. But I've never been so scared
that I wasn't ready... never worried about
forgetting lyrics. I make sure I have it
before I do it."

They soon started doing professional
dates. Local gigs gave way to larger halls in
distant cities. Joe Jackson spent his
weekends as chauffeur, road manager,
agent and coach.

Michael was taught how to handle a
microphone and use a stage. It was work
–not fun. Rules were rigid. Grades had to
be kept up, even with five shows a night, or
the bad student would get pulled off the
road.

Soon they were in the major cities,
performing with some of the biggest names
in soul music of the day: Chi-Lites, the
Temptations, Jackie Wilson, Etta James,
the O'Jays and Gladys Knight and the
Pips.

According to *Rolling Stone's* Gerri
Hirshey, "Michael's kindergarten was the
basement of the Apollo Theater in New
York's Harlem. He was too shy to actually
approach the performers the Jackson 5
opened for. He crept downstairs, along

passageways and walls and hid there, peering from behind the dusty flanks of old vaudeville sets while musicians tuned, smoked, played cards and divided barbecue. Climbing back to the wings, he stood in the protective folds of the musty maroon curtain, watching favorite acts, committing every double dip and every bump, snap, whip-it-back mike toss, to his inventory of night moves."

Michael says he will always remember watching James Brown perform. "He's so magic. I'd be in the wings when I was like six or seven. I'd sit there and watch him!"

"Everyone thinks we started at the top", says Marlon. "But we traveled around for five years before that –five brothers and two sisters– crammed into a Volkswagen van."

An obscure local label signed them and released two singles –both flopped.

But in 1968, popular record company Tamla Motown came into the picture. Popular legend says that Diana Ross discovered the boys. Gladys Knight claims she spotted them first but lacked the necessary clout at the company to get the right people to listen.

Bobby Taylor –a little known Motown musician– probably has the strongest claim. He says he arranged their first audition with Motown and it was then decided to attach Diana's name to the project to get more attention. Taylor, who was listed as one of the producers of the Jackson 5 debut album, says the decision didn't bother him in the least.

The most important thing is that they signed for Motown.

Motown was based in Detroit at the time –the Motor City– home of countless automobile factories. The record label manufactured hit records for acts such as Stevie Wonder, Marvin Gaye, Four Tops, Supremes and Diana Ross.

Very little has been said about the year between signing the Jackson 5's recording contract and the release of their first record. But it is safe to assume that Joe and Katherine Jackson's youngsters were getting groomed with all the polish and poise of the best finishing school in pop music.

They were showcased in a private party at the home of Motown founder, Berry Gordy.

"I remember it was the biggest place we'd ever seen", recalls Jackie. "His backyard was like a golf course and he had an indoor swimming pool. He had us entertain at a party and most of the Motown artists were there. That's what really scared us. We were up there doing their songs!"

Their first single, in 1970, 'I Want You Back', was more than just a hit. It was an aural steamroller. It took off like a rocket and exploded with a nervous, frenetic pace that wouldn't let up. Its energy and freshness was made irresistible by the desperate passion of Michael's vocal. Here was a boy screaming for mercy as if his life depended on it. It reached the parts other records couldn't reach.

It not only shot to number one in America, registering sizable hits around the world, but it ignited the fuse on the most explosive talents of the past decade and a half.

The record sold two million copies. At the time Jackie was 18, Tito was 16, Jermaine was 15, Marlon was 12 and Michael was a seasoned veteran at the age of 11.

And it was only the beginning.

All their early singles were million sellers –'I Want You Back', 'ABC', 'The Love You Save' and 'I'll Be There' sold four million each. They quickly established themselves as the bestselling act in Motown's history.

Jacksonmania had arrived, and on a scale not seen since the Beatles. The teeny magazines couldn't get enough of them, while the inner sleeves of their albums offered to sell 'Giant-Sized Photo Posters' and 'Personal Soul-Mate Kits'. There were also stickers, photo albums, magazines, portraits and stationery.

Despite all the success there was nothing fabricated about the Jackson 5 themselves –they were pure talent, and their stage show (for which they were augmented by two cousins, Ronnie Rancifer on electric piano and Johnny Jackson, making it an entirely family affair) was pure electricity.

The only problem they had was school.

"Most of our life we had private schooling", Michael recalls. "I only went to one public school in my life (in Gary). I tried another one here (Los Angeles), but it didn't work, because we'd be in our class and a bunch of fans would break into the classroom, or we'd come out of school and there'd be a bunch of kids waiting to take our pictures and stuff like that. We stayed at that school a whole week. One week! That's all we could take. The rest was private school with other entertainment kids or stars' kids, where you wouldn't have to be hassled."

By Christmas 1971 the Jackson 5 were one of the biggest recording acts in the world. Having sung all the major hits, it was inevitable that Michael should begin a solo career.

'Got To Be There' was the title of his debut album and single in 1972. Both sold like everything else this remarkable singer had put his voice to. The follow up singles 'Rockin' Robin', 'Ain't No Sunshine' and 'Ben' all hit the top of the charts.

A cartoon show, based on the boys from Gary, Indiana, served only to intensify the interest in Michael and the Jackson 5.

His biggest solo single on Motown was 'Ben' –the title track to the movie. The film was a sequel to 'Willard'. Both deal with a frustrated boy's power over a pack of rats, led by 'Ben'. The song –a beautiful ballad– won a Golden Globe award.

But this was a peak and the only way to go was down. Motown became increasingly out of touch with the creative needs of Joe Jackson's boys. The Jackson 5 were quickly becoming old hat.

The brothers moved into the easy listening world of Las Vegas and then began to sink without trace.

There was only one way to stop the decline. Since they felt Motown wouldn't let them choose their songs, play their instruments on record, choose their producers or record songs that weren't from the Motown vaults, they signed a deal with Epic records in 1976.

There were two sacrifices. First, Motown owned the name Jackson 5 and they had to become The Jacksons. Second, Jermaine, who'd married Hazel Gordy (daughter of Motown chief, Berry) three years previously, decided he'd stay with Motown.

"I was camping with Barry White and his wife", recalls Jermaine. "When I came back my father told me to come over to the house without Hazel. I knew something was wrong. I went to his room and on the bed were all the contracts from CBS/Epic already signed by my brothers. I just said I'm not going.

"I just believe that if it was meant for me it would have happened in a nicer way."

The move was just what the doctor ordered. The first single, 'Enjoy Yourself', sold a million worldwide. The second, 'Show You The Way To Go', was their first British number one.

By now, Randy had been brought in on bongos, to bring them back up to a complement of five.

They slowly eased themselves into writing and producing for themselves. By the time of their third Epic album in 1978, 'Destiny', they had finally released, for the first time, an album, which they were responsible for in all its aspects. It went double platinum. The Jacksons were back!

Now that The Jacksons could stand on their own two feet, without the Motown nest, it was time to spread their wings. Michael flew straight to Hollywood.

As early as 1971, Michael had confessed that he'd wanted to appear in motion pictures. Now he was given his chance.

The film version of the Broadway smash 'The Wiz' –a black version of 'The Wizard Of Oz'– was the most expensive black film ever produced. Not only that, but at $30 million, it was the most costly movie musical ever filmed in Hollywood.

Michael was to play the Scarecrow who looks to the newspaper clippings his head is stuffed with for ideas. His co-stars included Diana Ross, Richard Pryor and the legendary Lena Horne. Its director was the vastly experienced Sidney Lumet and its musical director was Quincy Jones –a man who was to play a vital role in Michael's future.

For Michael 'The Wiz' represented the fufillment of a life-long ambition. "Doing 'The Wiz' was an incredible experience. It was always something I wanted to do, because I had always loved the movie, and fell in love with the Scarecrow. I saw the play six times."

However, before filming could begin, Michael was taken ill. "I had a lung attack on the beach on the Fourth of July. I couldn't breathe. They had to rush me to the emergency hospital. The doctor said it was pneumothorax; bubbles on the lungs. Mostly slim people have it, the doctor said. He said there was a little bit of pleurisy there too. It reminded me that Buddy Ebsen was supposed to be the Tin Man in the original 'Wizard Of Oz', and he broke down sick before the thing."

Michael's thinness (his five foot nine frame weighs a mere 105 pounds) didn't help his stamina. But his professionalism made him turn up on the set on time.

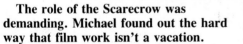

The role of the Scarecrow was demanding. Michael found out the hard way that film work isn't a vacation.

"I spent four hours a day for five months getting made-up, and it was well worth every minute. Man, that was painful," he says. "I'd finish a day's shooting in all the stuff, and then I'd leave the set with my skin all blotched and marked, and my eyes red and sore. There'd be fans outside and they'd point at me and say, 'Hey, that guy's on drugs –look what it's doing to him!' I'd explain that I never touch drugs, that it was just make-up for the movie, but I don't think they believed me. Sometimes I would go home in costume and make-up and the people would say, 'Trick or treat!' That was beautiful!"

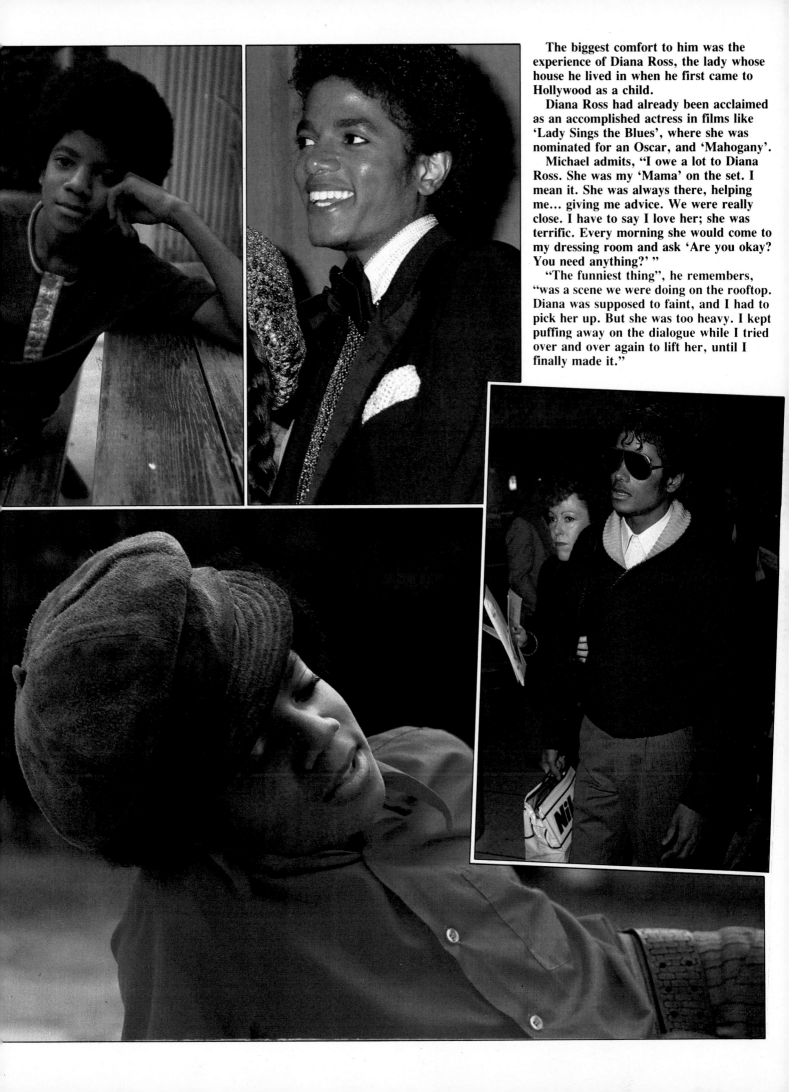

The biggest comfort to him was the experience of Diana Ross, the lady whose house he lived in when he first came to Hollywood as a child.

Diana Ross had already been acclaimed as an accomplished actress in films like 'Lady Sings the Blues', where she was nominated for an Oscar, and 'Mahogany'.

Michael admits, "I owe a lot to Diana Ross. She was my 'Mama' on the set. I mean it. She was always there, helping me... giving me advice. We were really close. I have to say I love her; she was terrific. Every morning she would come to my dressing room and ask 'Are you okay? You need anything?' "

"The funniest thing", he remembers, "was a scene we were doing on the rooftop. Diana was supposed to faint, and I had to pick her up. But she was too heavy. I kept puffing away on the dialogue while I tried over and over again to lift her, until I finally made it."

The film wasn't the monster hit everybody expected. It made respectable money but critics were unanimous in denouncing the film as suffocating in its own lavishness. The sparkle that made the stage show such an emotional experience was missing.

Despite this Michael was commended on his believable performance and had Hollywood clamoring to put the 'Wiz' kid onto the silver screen. He had created a Scarecrow to charm and beguile from his fabled wellspring of innocence and fantasy.

The film had made him a respected actor, increased his status within the Hollywood community and, most importantly, introduced Michael to Quincy Jones –a union that was to produce his magic albums 'Off The Wall' and 'Thriller!'

1979 was the 10th anniversary of The Jacksons and there was a tour to celebrate it. But it had been four years since Michael had released a solo album, and he was getting anxious to resume his solo recording career.

"I want to show that I can make it on my own", he exclaimed, "that my talent doesn't depend on anyone else. I have a responsibility to myself to do that. I guess every kid feels that way.

"The songs I do with the group are different from what I sing as a solo artist. I love ballads. A funky rock and roll song can be number one for three weeks, then you won't hear anything about it. A good ballad –'Mona Lisa', 'Moon River'– will last forever. I can be different and it's nice to have something to do and to look forward to that's different. It keeps me from going too crazy."

This album was going to be Michael's first while being totally in the driver's seat. He'd proved himself as a songwriter and producer on his brothers' 'Destiny' album, so it was all down to him.

The first problem was to get a producer.

"After we finished 'The Wiz', I called Quincy Jones to ask if he knew of any great producers for my album", he remembers. "He started thinking and said, 'I'll tell you what... why don't you let me do it?' Boy, was I excited. I never expected Quincy to produce my album, because he's so busy and in such demand. But I'm grateful that he decided to do it!"

Quincy recalls being pleasantly surprised by Michael when working on 'The Wiz'.

"I saw another side", he says. "Watching him in the context of being an actor, I saw a lot of things about him as a singer that rang a lot of bells. I saw a depth that was never apparent, and a commitment. I saw that Michael was growing up."

The album also marked the first time Michael worked with Paul McCartney –the partnership has since dueted on 'The Girl Is Mine' on Michael's 'Thriller!' album, and 'Say Say Say' and 'The Man' on Paul's 'Pipes Of Peace' LP.

Michael explains how it came about: "I was at a party on comedian Harold Lloyd's

estate in Los Angeles. Paul, Linda and I were having our picture taken and he said he'd written a song for me. He started singing 'Girlfriend' to me. I thought it was great so we switched phone numbers. I never got it together with him. The next time I heard it was on Paul's 'London Town' album. One day I was at Quincy Jones' house and he said he had a great song for me and played me 'Girlfriend'! he laughs.

"It was an ambition of mine to return the favor. I found him very professional. We have a lot in common. We're both fans of old cartoons, like those of MGM and Disney."

Jones recalls one particular incident with Michael, "I had a song I'd been saving for Michael called 'She's Out Of My Life'. Michael heard it, and it clicked. But when he sang it, he would cry. Every time we did it, I'd look up at the end and Michael would be crying. I said, 'We'll come back in two weeks and do it again, and maybe it won't tear you up as much'. Come back, and he started to get tearful. So we left it in."

'Off The Wall' was a record breaker. It sold 13 million copies worldwide. It became the first solo album to have four top 10 hits in America and Britain– 'Don't Stop 'Til You Get Enough', 'Off The Wall', 'Rock With You' and 'She's Out Of My Life'.

Suddenly, Michael Jackson was the hottest male recording star in the world!

1980 saw the release of The Jacksons' album 'Triumph' which coasted in on the new Jacksonmania wave. It spawned another four hits worldwide.

The same year Hollywood Boulevard's famous 'Walk Of Fame' added the Jackson's star to the legendary walkway. Michael and his brothers were getting bigger than the music world.

In 1981 Michael and his brothers launched a 39 city tour of America. But Michael admitted that this would probably be his last tour. He was fed up with everything about it, except for being on stage. It appears that the only place he feels comfortable is under the spotlights.

"I still want to make records, but I also want to do movies. That's how I want to spend my time the next few years."

Throughout Michael's solo career, rumors have flown around as to whether or not he's going to leave his brothers. Those that asked the question in the wake of the hugely successful 'Off The Wall' and 'Thriller' albums get an evasive answer.

He told Ebony magazine "Yes and no". He's told others that he tries to be guided by God and to do things when the time is right.

"I think the fans would be concerned... and to see a split like that would break their hearts. Especially when groups start changing their members... they lose originality and I'd really hate that...

"I let nature take its course. I let be what must be and if that is to come then it's going to happen, because there are so many things I do want to do. I want to explore, experiment and branch out to do different things and it is always a time problem."

During 1982 Michael was involved in three different recording projects.

He wrote and produced Diana Ross' 'Muscles'; he narrated the storybook album 'ET –The Extra-Terrestrial' and recorded his second Epic solo album 'Thriller'.

One of the first things he did for 'Thriller' was his duet with Paul McCartney, 'The Girl Is Mine', plus two songs for Paul's album.

"We're fighting over a girl in the song and it came out beautifully", he commented at the time. "There's a rap at the end when we're fighting over her. It's funny. I was coming back from England after working on Paul's album, zooming along in Concorde, and this song popped into my head. I said, 'Hey, that's perfect for Diana!' I didn't have a tape recorder or anything, so I had to suffer for three hours. Soon as I got home I whipped that baby on tape."

The song was 'Muscles' –a top 20 hit which went on to be nominated for a Grammy Award.

Steven Spielberg's 'ET – The Extra-Terrestrial' (the movie) was an instant smash all over the world. It reportedly made Spielberg half a million dollars a DAY.

But the cuddly alien has nothing on Michael Jackson according to Spielberg.

"If ET didn't come to Elliott, he would have come to Michael Jackson's house. Michael is one of the last living innocents who is in complete control of his life. I've never seen anybody like Michael. He's an emotional child star."

Michael was equally enamored by 'ET'. "The first time I saw 'ET', I melted through the whole thing", he says. "The second time, I cried like crazy. And then, when doing the narration album, I felt I was there with them, like behind a tree or something, watching everything that happened."

So great was Michael's involvement that Spielberg found his narrator crying in the darkened studio when it got to the part where the alien is dying. Finally, Spielberg and producer Quincy Jones decided to run with it and let Michael's voice break. Fighting those feelings would be counter – productive– something Jones had discovered while producing 'She's Out Of My Life'.

In December 1982 Epic finally released 'Thriller!' The face of pop and soul music hasn't been the same since.

'Thriller!' is the phenomenon of recording history. In the 15 months since its release it has sold 28 million copies worldwide. There have also been 20 million singles sold from the album. Michael Jackson has received over 100 gold and platinum records. He's had seven top 10 singles from the album in America, which beats his previous record of four. He's had five UK singles in the top 11.

Sales of the album are such that it's the biggest selling solo album ever. And it's about to top the two biggest albums, both double soundtracks, 'Saturday Night Fever' and 'Grease'.

Michael Jackson was already the king of the entertainment world. His records were being played constantly around the world. But what brought him the adoration of the world were his staggering videos.

It was the breathtaking 'Billie Jean', a number one virtually everywhere, that was the first on film.

Here's an eye-witness report from the set.

"Michael Jackson is sitting in the dressing room. He sits very quietly, staring into the mirror. His face is soft and delicately boned. His brown eyes have the big, dewey-eyed quality of Bambi. Like the fawn and his beloved 'ET', Michael Jackson is alone in a crowded room.

"Conversations dart around the room but Michael takes no notice –happy to live in his dream world. Talk to him direct and he'll answer you– quietly and politely. His voice is high but velvet smooth. You have to strain to hear his words. The exchange finished he retreats back into his world.

"Michael is called onto the set. He has to sing directly into the camera. He takes up his starting position. The assistant editor has uttered his last 'Schh!' All eyes are on Michael. The tape starts...

"He takes two beats to relax his body into the beat and then... he explodes.

"His body tenses and the energy is shot out from his wiry frame like a bullet. He faces the camera and spits out the lyrics –his voice can be heard over the deafening playback. Michael grips his left sleeve with his right hand and jerks it upwards.

"He growls the chorus to the camera. He doesn't dance so much as glide. He launches into one of his famous spins –three turns in succession.

"It's the end of the take. Everybody applauds. They all know they've seen a performance. Michael is glowing with the exhilaration of his efforts. He's back in the spotlight and he knows he's home."

'Beat It' was similarly epic. Instead of a song of wrongful accusal this is a mini-version of 'West Side Story'. A 1980s update on urban violence and inner-city aggression set against the searing guitar of Eddie Van Halen.

It featured the most stunning choreography and imagery yet seen in a video and rightfully claimed all the video prizes of 1983. It became the summer's most-shown video. At $100,000 cost, it should have been.

But still the Jackson flair for visual interpretation wasn't taxed. He was saving it for a 13-minute epic impression of his 'Thriller!' single. The track based on horror motifs included a ghoulish 'rap' by veteran spinechiller Vincent Price. The film was directed by Jon 'American Werewolf In London' Landis.

Everything was here, thrills, chills, laughs and love. Werewolves, ghouls and zombies popped their corpses to some of the best dance sequences ever seen. There were haunted houses, creepy-crawly cemeteries and some of the best visual gags this side of a Mel Brooks film. It was bliss.

Naturally, it was the favorite to win the 'Best Short Film' Oscar.

And the videos didn't stop there. He also appeared in the film for his 'Say Say Say' duet with Paul McCartney. They played a pair of lovable rogues around the turn of the century who conned people with an excellent line in street patter but gave the pickings to orphanages.

The video was romantic and whimsical and contained a charm that was hard to argue with.

But it hasn't all been plain sailing for Michael. While filming a commercial for Pepsi Cola with his brothers, now with Jermaine back in the fold, his hair lacquer caught alight when he stepped too close to some fireworks. The singer received second degree burns to the crown of his head and the back of his neck and head.

His doctor says that a small skin graft is necessary to cover a small area that has remained bald.

The accident happened at the Shrine Auditorium, Los Angeles, on January 27 1984. A month later he returned there in a blaze of glory when he scooped an unprecedented eight Grammy Awards, beating Simon and Garfunkel's 'Bridge Over Troubled Waters' total, set in 1970, by one.

'Beat It' was voted Record Of The Year and 'Thriller!' Album Of The Year. He also won awards for Best Pop Vocal Performance –'Thriller', Best Rock Vocal, Male Rhythm and Blues Vocal, Rhythm and Blues Song– 'Billie Jean', Producer of The Year –'Billie Jean', which he co-produced with Quincy Jones, and Best Children's Record –'ET'.

"Of all the awards I've got, I'm most proud of this one", said Michael as he accepted his 'ET' honor. "Children are a great inspiration."

The total equaled the amount he walked off with at the American Music Awards a few months before, which included two awards for the 'Beat It' video.

While the public image of Michael Jackson is of a dynamic performer who can send shockwaves of energy through any audience, his private life is conducted with extreme caution.

Michael suffers from shyness, not the sort that gets you tongue-tied, but the type that cripples any contact with other human beings. He lives a secluded life behind the high-powered security that his money can afford.

His home in Encino is a fortress to keep the hordes of fans out. He is a virtual recluse who spends much of his income on his favorite pastimes so he'll never have to leave his home.

He's a strict vegetarian and health food disciple. In fact, his mother worries that he seems to live on little more than air. As far as she can tell, her son has no interest in food. He admits that if he didn't have to eat to stay alive, he wouldn't.

The only restaurant he visits is a slightly run-down health food place in Los Angeles where the owners prepare his favorite dishes. Even then, they have to get rid of the other customers before Michael will come in.

He's made his home into a personal

fantasy-land. His fear of over-zealous fans forces him to drive miles out of his way to avoid being seen on a crowded motorway. He goes to Disneyland through the backdoor, or when it's closed, to use his favorite rides. He has a $500 a day suite there.

He's now building some of his favorite rides, with the help of Disney technicians, in his private rooms. There, the experts are creating the set of a swashbuckling pirate film, with lifelike dummies that constantly battle.

He's installed a film screening room and he's adding a gymnasium and a videogames room.

He doesn't drink, he doesn't smoke and has never used drugs.

Every Sunday he fasts. He explains: "It flushes out the system, cleans out the colon. To make it work you have to do it properly. That's the sewer valve of the body. You have to keep that clean like you clean the outside of your body. All the impurities come out of the system because you're not clean inside. It comes out in pimples, or disease."

He dances himself to exhaustion on Sundays. His mother usually finds him on the floor crying with happiness after a session.

But how does he write music?

"I wake up from dreams and go, 'Wow! Put this down on paper!' The whole thing is strange. You hear the words, everything is right there in front of your face. And you say to yourself, 'I'm sorry, I just didn't write this. It's there already'. I feel that somewhere, someplace, it's all been done, and I'm the courier bringing it into the world."

He has a private zoo where he keeps two fawns, two swans, two dogs, two parrots, four cockatoos, a sheep, a peacock, a llama

called Louie and an eight foot boa constrictor called Muscles. Sister Janet says Michael has recently ordered a baby giraffe, while she wants a chimpanzee.

Aside from his highly protected appearances, sometimes escorted by Brooke Shields to friends' parties and awards ceremonies the only other time Michael ventures out into the real world is to attend Jehovah's Witness meetings with his mother.

Most evenings he passes the time watching children's cartoon films. His favorites are Disney, Bugs Bunny, old MGM ones, and the Three Stooges.

Old movies are another of Michael's passions.

He admits to living in a fantasy world. He loves shop window mannequins. He likes to imagine conversations with them. They are the friends he never had in his isolated upbringing. He is having a room in his new house filled with them.

But the obvious clue to his personality and how he sees himself is that his bedroom wall is covered with pictures of Peter Pan. Jane Fonda, a close friend, talks: "Michael reminds me of the walking wounded. He's an extremely fragile person. I remember driving with him one day, 'God, Michael, I wish I could find a movie for you'. And suddenly I knew. I said, 'I know what you've got to do. It's Peter Pan'. Tears welled up in his eyes and he said, 'Why did you say that?' with this ferocity. I said, 'I realize you're Peter Pan'."

Michael Jackson is the boy from Never Never Land. He can bring joy, fun and adventure. He can tingle every spine with the merest inflection of voice. He can pump tears from the toughest skin. But he lives by the legend –"All children, except one, grow up."